ARISTOPHANES

The Frogs

Translated by
David Barrett

PENGUIN BOOKS

PENGUIN CLASSICS

UK | USA | Canada | Ireland | Australia
India | New Zealand | South Africa

Penguin Classics is part of the Penguin Random House group of companies
whose addresses can be found at global.penguinrandomhouse.com.

This edition first published in Penguin Classics 2016
001

Translation copyright © David Barrett, 1964

Set in 10/14.5 pt Baskerville 10 Pro
Typeset by Jouve (UK), Milton Keynes
Printed in Great Britain by Clays Ltd, St Ives plc

A CIP catalogue record for this book is available from the British Library

ISBN: 978-0-241-25038-9

www.greenpenguin.co.uk

MIX
Paper from
responsible sources
FSC® C018179

Penguin Random House is committed to a
sustainable future for our business, our readers
and our planet. This book is made from Forest
Stewardship Council® certified paper.

Characters

DIONYSUS *patron god of drama*

XANTHIAS *his slave*

HERACLES (*Hercules*)

A CORPSE

CHARON *ferryman of the dead*

AEACUS *doorkeeper of Hades*

MAID *to Persephone*

Two LANDLADIES

AN ELDERLY SLAVE *servant to Pluto*

EURIPIDES *the dramatist*

AESCHYLUS *the dramatist*

PLUTO

THE CHORUS: *a band of Initiates, old and young*

CHORUS OF FROGS

Aristophanes

A CASTANET GIRL

CORPSE-BEARERS, SLAVES, DANCING-GIRLS, DIS-
TINGUISHED RESIDENTS OF HADES, *etc.*

Act One

SCENE I: *The action begins on the outskirts of Athens, and ends in Hades. A building in the background represents, first, the house of* HERACLES, *and later, the palace of* PLUTO

[*Enter* DIONYSUS *and his slave* XANTHIAS. *The god, here represented as a paunchy but still handsome middle-aged man-about-town, is dressed in the yellow robe appropriate to a Dionysiac festival, which resembles a woman's garment, and in the buskins or high laced-up boots of a tragic actor – these also have a somewhat feminine look. Over the robe he wears a lion-skin, and in his hand is an enormous club: he has attempted to disguise himself as* HERACLES. *He is on foot, but his slave is riding a donkey. The slave is laden with bundles of bedding and other packages, many of which are suspended from a stout pole which rests across his shoulder.*]

3

XANTHIAS [*surveying the audience unenthusiastically*]:
What about one of the old gags, sir? I can always
get a laugh with those.

DIONYSUS: All right, Xanthias, but don't just keep
saying 'Cor, what a load!' I've got enough to put
up with as it is.

XANTHIAS: Something a bit wittier, eh, sir?

DIONYSUS: Yes, but don't start off with 'Oh, my poor
neck!'

XANTHIAS: Oh. Pity. What *can* I give them, then? –
Oh, you mean something really *funny*?

DIONYSUS: Yes. And I don't mean just shifting that
pole about and saying you want to *ease yourself*
of a –

XANTHIAS: Well, how about this:

'If nobody will take away my pack
I'll let a fart and blow it off my back.'

DIONYSUS: Keep that one till I really need an emetic.

XANTHIAS: Do you mean to say I've been lugging
all these props around and now I'm not even
allowed to get a laugh out of them? It's the regular
thing, I tell you. Phrynichus, Lysis, Ameipsias, all
the popular writers do it. Comic porter scene.
There's one in every comedy.

DIONYSUS: Well, there's not going to be one in this one. Every time I go to a show and have to sit through one of these scintillating comic routines, I come away more than a year older.

XANTHIAS: Oh, my poor neck, and all for nothing.

DIONYSUS: Anyway, things have come to a pretty pass, I'm not sure that it isn't sacrilege or something, when I, Dionysus, son of Jug, have to struggle along on foot, while this pampered creature is allowed to ride, so that he won't tire himself out carrying the luggage.

XANTHIAS: I like that. I *am* carrying the luggage, aren't I?

DIONYSUS: Of course not, you're riding.

XANTHIAS: Never mind, I'm carrying the luggage just the same.

DIONYSUS: I don't get that.

XANTHIAS: No, I've got it. And I'm telling you, it weighs a packet.

DIONYSUS: But the donkey's carrying all that.

XANTHIAS: Oh, is he? You ask my shoulders!

DIONYSUS: Ah, well, in that case the donkey's not being much use to you, is he? You'd better change places with him.

XANTHIAS: Oh, for heaven's sake! If only I'd been in that sea-battle, I'd be a free man now. And if I got my hands on you . . .

DIONYSUS: Come on, get down off that moke. Here we are, if I'm not mistaken. This is where we pay our first call. You see, I've walked the whole way.

[*While* XANTHIAS *disentangles himself and his burdens from the donkey,* DIONYSUS *approaches the front door and knocks cautiously. There is no response.*]

Hallo there!

[*There is still no response. Remembering his disguise, he swings his club, hitting the door with a resounding crash.*]

Hallo, there! Slave! Open up!

HERACLES [*within*]: Ho, ho, who smites my door? Some Centaur, doubtless.

[*The door opens, and* HERACLES *himself appears. He stares in amazement at Dionysus.*]

What . . . who . . . ?

[*In a convulsion of mirth and amazement he collapses to the ground.*]

DIONYSUS: There, did you notice?

XANTHIAS: Notice what?

DIONYSUS: How I frightened him.

XANTHIAS: Mistook you for a madman, I expect, sir.

HERACLES: Oh, by Demeter, I can't stop laughing.
[*He struggles to his feet and retires into the house.*]

DIONYSUS: Come back a minute, old boy, there's something I want to ask you.

HERACLES [*returning*]: Sorry, old man, but really I can't help it. A lion-skin over a yellow nightdress! What's the idea? Why the buskins? Why the club? What's your regiment?

DIONYSUS: Well, it's like this, you see. I was on Cleisthenes' ship –

HERACLES: Clei—! [*He splutters.*] Saw a good bit of action, I expect, one way or another?

DIONYSUS: Oh, yes, we sank twelve enemy ships. Or was it thirteen?

HERACLES: What, just the two of you?

DIONYSUS: Yes, by Apollo.

XANTHIAS: And then I woke up.

DIONYSUS: Well, as I was saying, I was on the ship and one day – I was reading the *Andromeda* at the time – do you know, I suddenly felt the most passionate longing – you can't imagine how I longed –

7

HERACLES: For a woman.

DIONYSUS: Not a bit of it.

HERACLES: A boy? [DIONYSUS *shakes his head.*] A man, then?

DIONYSUS: Oh, come, come, really!

HERACLES: You did say Cleisthenes was a friend of yours?

DIONYSUS: Don't laugh at me, old man, this is deadly serious. I'm in a terrible state. *Consumed* with desire.

HERACLES: Yes, but what sort of desire, my dear fellow?

DIONYSUS: Ah, you wouldn't understand. Let me put it this way. Have you ever felt a sudden craving for – let's say – pea soup?

HERACLES: Ah, now you're talking! When do I *not* have a craving for pea soup?

DIONYSUS: Are you with me, or would you care for another illustration?

HERACLES: No, no, pea soup will do nicely. I understand perfectly. [*He smacks his lips.*]

DIONYSUS: Well, that is the kind of desire that I feel for – Euripides.

HERACLES: But he's – a corpse! I mean to say!

DIONYSUS: No one on earth can stop me from going
  to seek him out.

HERACLES: What, down to Hades?

DIONYSUS [*dramatically*]: And deeper still, if need be.

HERACLES: With what object, may I ask?

DIONYSUS: I need a poet who can *write*. There are
  only two kinds of poet nowadays, the slick and the
  dead.

HERACLES: Oh, come! What about Sophocles' son,
  young Iophon?

DIONYSUS: He's the only one left that's any good,
  and even then I'm not sure.

HERACLES: Why not fetch back Sophocles, if you
  must have one of them back? He was much better
  than Euripides.

DIONYSUS: Not till I've seen how Iophon manages
  without his father to help him. Besides, Euripides
  will be readier to sneak away with me, he's a much
  more slippery customer; whereas Sophocles, well,
  he always took life as it came – he's probably taking
  death as it comes too.

HERACLES: And what's happened to Agathon?

DIONYSUS: Gone, gone; he too has left me. [*He sighs.*]
  A good poet; his friends will miss him.

HERACLES: Where has he gone, poor fellow?

DIONYSUS: To the Banquet of the Blessèd. Specially laid on by the King of Macedon.

HERACLES: And what about Xenocles?

DIONYSUS: Oh, Xenocles be hanged.

HERACLES: And Pythangelus?

XANTHIAS: Never a word about little me. And look at my poor shoulder, it'll never be the same again.

HERACLES: But surely there are dozens of these young whipper-snappers churning out tragedies these days: for sheer verbiage, if that's what you want, they leave Euripides standing.

DIONYSUS: Small fry, I assure you, insignificant squeakers and twitterers, like a lot of swallows. A disgrace to their art. If ever they *are* granted a chorus, what does their offering at the shrine of Tragedy amount to? One cock of the hind leg and they've pissed themselves dry. You never hear of them again. I defy you to find a really seminal poet among the whole crowd of them: someone who can coin a fine resounding phrase.

HERACLES: What do you mean, seminal?

DIONYSUS: A poet who can produce something really audacious, like 'Ether, the residence of Zeus', or 'the foot of Time', or that business about the tongue being able to perjure itself and the heart not being committed, you remember?

HERACLES: You like that sort of thing?

DIONYSUS: I'm crazy about it.

HERACLES: But that stuff's all eyewash, you must see that.

DIONYSUS: 'Seek not within my mind to dwell,' as the poet says. You've got a house of your own.

HERACLES: What's more, it's downright immoral.

DIONYSUS: When I want advice about *food*, old man, I'll come to you. Meanwhile –

XANTHIAS: Never a word about little me.

DIONYSUS: But to come to the point – I see you're looking at my lion-skin. Well, I took the liberty, seeing that you travelled in those parts when you went down after Cerberus – well, I wondered if perhaps you could give me a few tips: any useful contacts down there, where you get the boat, which are the best eating-houses, bread shops, wine shops, knocking shops . . . And which places have the fewest bugs.

XANTHIAS: I might as well not exist.

HERACLES: You don't seriously intend to go down there? You're crazy!

DIONYSUS: Never mind that, just give me a simple answer: which is the quickest way to Hades? I want a route that's not too warm and not too cold.

HERACLES: Let me see now. You could go via Rope and Gibbet: that's a very quick way, if you don't mind hanging around for a bit, to begin with.

DIONYSUS: Don't give me a pain in the neck!

HERACLES: Well, there's a good short way of executing the journey, via Pestle and Mortar. That's used a lot these days – you can just *pound* along.

DIONYSUS: Hemlock?

HERACLES: That's right.

DIONYSUS: Now you're giving me cold feet!

HERACLES: You want a way that just goes straight down?

DIONYSUS: Exactly. You see, I'm not much of a walker.

HERACLES: Oh, a *runner*! Well – you know the tower in the Potters' Quarter? Well, just go and hang on to the top of that tower, and watch the start of the torch race. And when they shout 'One, two, three, *off!*' – well, off you go.

DIONYSUS: Where to?

HERACLES: To the bottom.

DIONYSUS: Oh, no, just think – all those lovely brains. I'm not going that way.

HERACLES: Which way *do* you want to go, then?

DIONYSUS: The way you went.

HERACLES: Ah, but that's a long trip. The first thing you come to is a great big bottomless lake.

DIONYSUS: How do I get across?

HERACLES: There's an old ferryman who'll take you across in a tiny boat, about so big, for two obols.

DIONYSUS: Amazing what you can do with two obols these days!

HERACLES: Ah, yes, it was Theseus who introduced the idea down there: an Athenian, you see. Well, after that you come to the snakes and the wild beasts – thousands of 'em.

DIONYSUS: Now, it's no good trying to scare me off.

HERACLES: And then you come to the Great Muck Marsh and the Eternal River of Dung – you'll find some pretty unsavoury characters floundering about in that: people who have wronged a guest, or had a pretty boy and failed to pay him, or knocked their mothers about, or punched their fathers on the jaw, or committed perjury –

DIONYSUS: Or learnt to dance the jelly-wobble, like Cinesias, or published a play by Morsimus, or –

HERACLES: After that you'll hear the sound of flute-playing and you'll come out into brilliant daylight, just like it is up here. Farther on you'll see plantations of myrtle, and happy bands of revellers, men and women, tripping around and clapping their hands and so on.

DIONYSUS: What on earth for?

HERACLES: Oh, those are the Initiates – been through the mystic rites and all that.

XANTHIAS: I'm going to stand up for *my* mystic rights, and have a sit down. [*He starts to divest himself of his numerous burdens.*]

HERACLES: They'll tell you anything you want to know; they're right on the road to Pluto's palace. Well, good-bye, old man, and the best of luck.

DIONYSUS: Don't worry, I'll be all right. Bye-bye, keep well!

[HERACLES *waves good-bye and goes indoors.*]
Now, you! Pick up all that baggage, and we'll get going.

XANTHIAS: I haven't even got it off yet.

[*He looks round for the donkey, but it has wandered off and is not seen again.*]

DIONYSUS: Come on, look sharp.

XANTHIAS: Now look, guvnor, have a heart! Look at all these stiffs they're carrying out. Might have been ordered specially.

[*Several corpses are carried in slow procession across the stage. Mournful music.*]

Go on, hire one of them to take your things down with him.

DIONYSUS: Supposing they won't?

XANTHIAS: Then I'll do it.

DIONYSUS: Well, all right. – Ah, here comes one, I'll ask him. Er – hullo, excuse me! Yes, you there! Stiff!

[*The* BEARERS *of the last litter come to a halt. The* CORPSE *sits up with a jerk.*]

Ah, would you do me a favour and take my baggage to blazes?

CORPSE: How many pieces?

DIONYSUS: Just these.

CORPSE: That'll be two drachmas.

DIONYSUS: Too much.

CORPSE: Bearers, proceed!

DIONYSUS: Hi, wait a minute! Can't we come to some arrangement?

CORPSE: Two drachmas, cash down, or nothing.

DIONYSUS [*counting out his small change*]: I can pay you nine obols.

CORPSE: I'd sooner live!

[*The* CORPSE *lies down again with a jerk, and is carried off.*]

XANTHIAS: Well, of all the stuck-up blighters. He'll come to a bad end. [*Resignedly*] All right, guvnor. Load me up again.

[DIONYSUS *helps him load up, and they begin to move on.*]

DIONYSUS: That's a good lad. Now, where's this ferry boat?

CHARON [*off*]: Yo, heave, ho! Yo, heave, ho!

[*The stage grows darker and more eerie.*]

XANTHIAS: Where are we?

DIONYSUS: This must be the lake he was talking about, and – ah! here comes the boat.

[CHARON *comes into view, propelling a small boat on wheels.*]

XANTHIAS: And *that* must be Charon.

DIONYSUS: Charon! [*No response.*] Charon!! Charon!!! [*No response.*] Well, he's not Charon much about *us*, is he?

CHARON: Any more for Lethe, Blazes, Perdition, or the Dogs? Come along now, any more for a nice restful trip to Eternity? No more worries, no more cares, makes a lovely break! [*To Dionysus*] Well, come along then, if you're coming.

DIONYSUS [*climbing in warily*]: Er – can I go to Hell?

CHARON: You can as far as I'm concerned.

DIONYSUS: Ah, splendid. Two, please.

CHARON: Sorry, sir, no slaves allowed. Not unless they fought in the sea-battle.

XANTHIAS: Exempted on medical grounds, I was. Weak sight.

CHARON: Well, you'll have to walk round.

XANTHIAS: Where shall I find you?

CHARON: Just past the Withering Stone, you'll find an inn. 'The Last Resting Place', they call it.

DIONYSUS: Got that?

XANTHIAS: I've got the creeps, that's what I've got. It's not my lucky day. [*He staggers off into the shadows.*]

CHARON: Sit to the oar. Any more for Lethe, Blazes – Here, what are you doing?

DIONYSUS: Sitting on the oar, like you said. But –

CHARON: I didn't say *on* the oar, you pot-bellied loon. This is where you sit, here on the cross-bench.

DIONYSUS: Like this?

CHARON: Yes. Now stretch your arms forward and take hold of the oar – that's right.

DIONYSUS: Like this?

CHARON: Don't talk so much: shove her off.

[CHARON *settles down comfortably in the stern, while* DIONYSUS *makes clumsy efforts to get the boat moving.*]

DIONYSUS: How do you expect me to drive this thing? I'm not a sea-going type.

CHARON: It's easy. Come on, man, get forward. Just a couple of strokes, and then you'll have the singing to help you. Lovely, it is.

DIONYSUS: Singing?

CHARON: Yes, the Frogswans. It's a treat.

DIONYSUS: Right: you start me off, then.

CHARON: I-i-i-n, OUT! I-i-i-n, OUT!

[*As soon as* DIONYSUS *has got his stroke adjusted to the tempo set by* CHARON, *the voices of the* FROG CHORUS *are heard off-stage, singing in an entirely different rhythm.*]

FROGS: Brekeke-kex, ko-ax, ko-ax,
        Ko-ax, ko-ax, ko-ax!
Oh we are the musical Frogs!
We live in the marshes and bogs!
Sweet, sweet is the hymn
That we sing as we swim,
And our voices are known
For their beautiful tone
When on festival days
We sing to the praise
Of the genial god –
And we don't think it odd
When the worshipping throng,
To the sound of our song,
ROLLS HOME through the marshes and bogs,
        Brekekex!
Rolls home through the marshes and bogs.

DIONYSUS:
I don't want to row any more,

FROGS: Brekekex!

DIONYSUS:
For my bottom is getting so sore.

FROGS: Brekekex!

DIONYSUS:

> And what do you care?
> You are nothing but air,
> And I find you a bit of a bore.

FROGS: Brekeke-kex, ko-ax, ko-ax,
> Ko-ax, ko-ax, ko-ax!
> Your remarks are offensive in tone,
> And we'd like to make some of our own.
> Our plantation of reeds
> For all musical needs
> In the very best circles is known.
> Should Apollo require
> A new bridge for his lyre,
> He comes to the Frogs
> Of the marshes and bogs;
> We've exactly the type
> That Pan needs for his pipe
> When he plays for our chorus;
> The Muses adore us!
> We're the rage on Parnassus,
> For none can surpass us
> In harmony, sweetness, and tone,

> Brekekex!
> In harmony, sweetness, and tone.

DIONYSUS:

> What a sweat! I'm all wet! What a bore!
> I'm so raw! I'm so sore! and what's more,
>> The blisters have come
>> On my delicate bum,
> Where I've never had blisters before.

– Any minute now and it'll join in the chorus.

FROGS: Brekeke-kex, ko-ax, ko-ax –

DIONYSUS: Listen, my melodious friends, put a sock in it, can't you?

FROGS:

> Ko-ax, ko-ax, ko-ax!
> What, silence our chorus? Ah, no!
> Let us sing as we sang long ago,
> When we splashed in the sun
> (Oh, wasn't it fun)
> 'Mid the weeds and the sedge
> At the pond's muddy edge.
> If it came on to rain
> We'd dive under again
> (To avoid getting soaked)

And still harder we croaked,
Till from under the slime
Our subaqueous rhyme
Bubbled out loud and clear
For all men to hear,
And burst with a plop at the top,
    Brepeplep!
And burst with a plop at the top.

DIONYSUS:

It's all this exertion, no doubt,
But I fancy that I am about
    To take over from you!

FROGS: We'll be sunk if you do!

DIONYSUS:

I shall burst if I don't, so look out!

FROGS: Brekeke-kex-ko-ax, ko-ax –
DIONYSUS: Ko-ax, ko-ax, ko-ax!
Now listen, you musical twerps,
I don't give a damn for your burps!

FROGS: Then we'll burp all the more,
Twice as loud as before,
Till our cavernous throats
Cannot hold all the notes

>   Of the ear-splitting song
>   That we'll chant all day long:

DIONYSUS [*getting in first*]:

>   Brekekex! Brekekex! Brekekex!
>   It's hopeless, you see:
>   You can never beat me!

FROGS: We shall see about that.

DIONYSUS:

>   You won't, and that's flat:
>   I'll go on till I bust –
>   Yes, all day if I must;
>   But I know I shall win in the end,
>   BREKEKEX!

>   [*He pauses: the Frogs are silent.*]

>   Yes, I *knew* I should win in the end.

CHARON: Whoa there, land ahoy! Ship your oars!

>   [*The boat grounds with a crash.*]

Well, here we are, sir; don't forget the ferryman.

DIONYSUS [*staggering ashore*]: Ah, yes, those two obols.

>   [*He pays the fare, and the boat moves off.*]

Xanthias! Where are you? Xanthias!

>   [*It is now quite dark. Ghostly shadows flit across the
>   stage. An owl hoots.*]

XANTHIAS: Coo-ee!

DIONYSUS: Come here!

XANTHIAS [*emerging from the shadows*]: You called, sir?

DIONYSUS: What's it like over here?

XANTHIAS: Very dark, sir. And very muddy, sir.

DIONYSUS: Any sign of those murderers and perjurers he told us about?

XANTHIAS: Use your eyes, sir.

DIONYSUS [*seeing the audience*]: By Jove, yes, I see them now. Well, what are we going to do?

XANTHIAS: We'd better be pushing on, guvnor. The place is full of 'orrible monsters, or so the gentleman said.

DIONYSUS: Yes, the old scoundrel – he was just piling on the horrors, to scare me off. Jealous, you know – a chap like me with a military record . . . Terribly sensitive about his exploits, old Heracles. I must say I rather hope we do meet something. One ought to slay a dragon or two on a trip like this, what?

XANTHIAS: Tsh! What's that noise?

DIONYSUS [*in a panic*]: Where's it coming from?

XANTHIAS: It's somewhere behind us.

DIONYSUS: Here, let me go in front.

XANTHIAS: No, it's in front of us!

DIONYSUS: On second thoughts, old man, you'd better go first.

XANTHIAS: There it is! Oh, what a dreadful monster!

DIONYSUS: W-what sort of a monster?

XANTHIAS: Horrible – it keeps on changing. It's sort of like a bull – no, now it's a mule! Wait a minute, it's changing again. [*He whistles.*] Oh, my, what a beautiful girl!

DIONYSUS: Here, let me past, quickly!

XANTHIAS: Oh, what a shame – it's stopped being a woman, it's turned into a dog.

DIONYSUS [*with a shudder*]: It must be the Empusa.

XANTHIAS: Her face is all lit up.

DIONYSUS: Has she got a copper leg?

XANTHIAS: Yes, I do believe you're right, sir. And the other one's made of cow dung.

DIONYSUS: Oh, where can I go?

XANTHIAS: Where can *I* go, come to that?

DIONYSUS [*appealing to the priest of Dionysus, who is sitting in the front row*]: Oh, mister priest, oh, protect me – oh, oh, help, help! Remember that drink we're going to have after the show!

XANTHIAS: Heracles, old man, we've had it.

DIONYSUS: Sh! Don't call me that, for heaven's sake: don't breathe that name down here.

XANTHIAS: Well, Dionysus, then.

DIONYSUS: No, no, that's even worse.

XANTHIAS [*to the spectre*]: Over that way! That's right! Now keep straight on!

   [DIONYSUS, *thinking these remarks are addressed to him, flees blindly through the auditorium.*]

No, no, not you! Come back! This way, guvnor!

DIONYSUS [*returning*]: What's happened?

XANTHIAS: It's all right now. We've weathered the storm. Or, as Hegelochus would say, the pillows heave no more. In other words, she's gone.

DIONYSUS: You're not kidding?

XANTHIAS: I swear it.

DIONYSUS: Swear it again.

XANTHIAS: Cross my heart.

DIONYSUS: You're quite sure?

XANTHIAS: She's gone, I tell you.

DIONYSUS [*airily*]: I must say she had me quite worried for a moment, Xanthias. Which of the gods do we have to thank for that little spot of bother, I wonder? Ether, the residence of Zeus? Or the Foot of Time? [*He laughs heartily at his own joke.*]

XANTHIAS: Tsh!

DIONYSUS [*in a panic again*]: What is it?

XANTHIAS: Listen, can't you hear it?

DIONYSUS: What?

XANTHIAS: Music. Flute-playing.

DIONYSUS: So it is. [*He sniffs the air.*] And a most mystical whiff of torches. Keep quiet, let's crouch down here and listen.

[*They conceal themselves. The sound of music comes nearer, and the* CHORUS *is heard chanting* 'Iacchos, Iacchos!']

XANTHIAS: These must be the happy bands of Initiates he told us about. Yes, they're singing the hymn to Iacchos, by that fellow Diagoras.

DIONYSUS: Yes, I think you're right. Let's keep quiet and make sure.

[*Enter, by torchlight, the* CHORUS OF INITIATES, *the men and the women entering in separate groups, each with a male leader.*]

CHORUS:

> Come, Iacchos, leave your temple,
> > Join your celebrants devout!
> Come and dance across the meadows,
> > Lead us in the mystic rout!

> Toss your head and swing the berries
>> On your myrtle crown so gay;
> Stamp and prance with feet delirious,
>> Whirling every qualm away.
>
> Here with dancing, songs, and laughter –
>> All the best of all the arts –
> We your worshippers await you:
>> Come, oh come! The revel starts!

[They dance, with suitable abandon, as the sacrificial meal is prepared and the wine cups filled.]

XANTHIAS [*mocking them*]: Oh, Persephone, Paragon of Perfection, oh, Divine Daughter of Demeter – what a wonderful smell of pork!

DIONYSUS: You'd better keep quiet, or you won't get so much as a sausage.

[The CHORUS resume their hymn. At the cue in the second line, the torches are raised and flare up, and a strange and beautiful light fills the stage.]

CHORUS:

> Call upon him, call Iacchos!
>> Raise the torches, wake the flame!
> See, at once the darkness scatters
>> As we shout the sacred name.

See, the meadows blaze! Iacchos,
   Day-star of our secret rite,
Comes to wake the mystic knowledge
   Born in us at dead of night,

Turning all to dance and movement,
   Setting souls and bodies free;
Aged knees shake off their stiffness
   In the rhythmic ecstasy.

Shine for us, and we will follow!
   Lead us on, our strength renew:
Young and old shall dance together
   'Mid the flowers, drenched with dew.

[*They dance again, and then sit down to partake of the sacrificial meat and wine. Meanwhile the two* LEADERS *pronounce the traditional warning to the uninitiated.*]

MEN'S LEADER:

Now all you bystanders, keep silent, we pray!
The holy procession proceeds on its way.
And all you outsiders who know not our rite,
Stay away from our revels and keep out of sight.

CHORUS: Stand away there, outsiders, you're not wanted here.

WOMEN'S LEADER:

We've no use for bounders who don't understand
The traditions of Comedy noble and grand;
Who snigger and leer till the festival's ended,
And find dirty meanings where none are intended.
CHORUS: Stand away there, outsiders, you're not
    wanted here.

MEN'S LEADER:

We don't want the leaders who fan party strife
When what we all need is a peaceable life;
Or the customs inspector from somewhere near by
Who's been smuggling out naval supplies on the sly.
CHORUS: Stand away there, outsiders, you're not
    wanted here.

WOMEN'S LEADER:

Oh we don't want the traitor who sides with the foe,
We don't want the soldier who lets the fort go;
The greedy official who's even prepared
To betray his own City, if suitably squared.
CHORUS: Stand away there, outsiders, you're not
    wanted here.

MEN'S LEADER:

Some people there are who, when guyed in a play,
Take it out on the poet by cutting his pay.

We've no use for them, nor for poets who bore us
And who get taken short in the middle of the
    chorus.

CHORUS: Stand away there, outsiders, you're not
    wanted here.

    [*The feasting over, the* CHORUS *group themselves for
    the ceremony, which consists of songs and dances in
    honour of Persephone, Demeter, and Iacchos.*]

MEN'S LEADER [*solemnly*]: Sing now, and let the fes-
    tival begin.

CHORUS:

    Now we're well fortified,
    Let's get into our stride;
To the sweet flow'ry meadow let's march off in pride;
    At distinguished bystanders
    We'll jest and we'll jeer;
It's the feast of the Goddess, we've nothing to fear.

    The praises we'll sing
    Of the Princess of Spring,
Who returns at this season salvation to bring;
    Though traitors endeavour
    Her plan to frustrate,
We know she will save us before it's too late.

WOMEN'S LEADER: And now, in a different strain, let us honour our Queen and Goddess Demeter, Bringer of Plenty, with a holy hymn.

CHORUS:

> Queen Demeter, stand before us,
> Smile upon your favourite Chorus!
> Grant that when we dance and play
> As befits your holy day,
> Part in earnest, part in jest,
> We may shine above the rest,
> And our play in all men's eyes
> Favour find, and win the prize.

MEN'S LEADER: Now with your songs call forth the youthful god, to join us in our dancing.

MEN:

Iacchos, Iacchos, lead on to the shrine!
Our hearts are on fire with your music divine!
Come, teach us to dance over hedgerows and stiles –
And to keep up the tempo for twelve blooming miles.

ALL:

Iacchos, Iacchos, dance on and we'll follow.

WOMEN:

Last night as we revelled from twilight to dawn
My clothes and my sandals to ribbons were torn.

It's the fault of the god, but perhaps his defence is
That it raises a laugh and cuts down the expenses.

ALL:

Iacchos, Iacchos, dance on and we'll follow.

MEN:

A girl I did spy as we sported and played:
A really remarkably pretty young maid.
She winked and she giggled, but what I liked best
Was the little pink titty that peeped from her vest.

ALL:

Iacchos, Iacchos, dance on and we'll follow.

XANTHIAS: Come to that, I wouldn't mind sporting
with her myself. Being a sociable sort of fellow,
and all that.

DIONYSUS: Come along, then, what are we waiting for?
[*They join in the ensuing dance, after which the*
CHORUS *halts, facing the audience, with* DIONYSUS
and XANTHIAS *now in the centre, and proceeds to
'jest and jeer' at notable members of the audience, as
promised in the hymn to Persephone.*]

CHORUS:

You've heard of Archedemus? Well, he's not renowned
for looks;

His parentage is doubtful, and he isn't on the books;
Yet up among the dead men he's the prince of all the
    crooks –
  It's the way they do things now.

Oh what's come over Cleisthenes? He looks so full
    of care;
He's lost his lovely boy-friend and his sad cries rend
    the air
As he wields a pair of tweezers on his last superfluous
    hair –
  It's the way they do things now.

Now Callias the naval man is at his best ashore,
Where he can show his seamanship in actions by the
    score:
And when they see his lion-skin the girls cry out for
    more –
  It's the way they do things now.

DIONYSUS:
Excuse me interrupting, but we're strangers here in
    Hell:
Can some kind person tell us, where does Master
    Pluto dwell?

CHORUS:

His house is not so distant, you can find it very well –
   It's just behind you now.

DIONYSUS:

Pick up the luggage, Xanthias, let's knock and take
      a chance.

XANTHIAS:

I'm tired of all this portering, I'd rather stay and
      dance.

Another time I hope you'll send your luggage in
      advance –
   It's the way they do things now.

   [DIONYSUS *and* XANTHIAS *return to their luggage
   as the* CHORUS *prepare for the procession.*]

MEN'S LEADER: Dance on then merrily through the
   flowery grove; let all that have part in our festival
   tread the sacred precinct of the Goddess.

WOMEN'S LEADER: And I will bear the holy torch for
   the girls and the women; let them dance to the
   glory of the Goddess, the whole night long.

   [*The* WOMEN *and their* LEADER *dance off.*]

MEN:

Let us hasten to the meadow, where the roses are so
  sweet,

And the little flowers grow in profusion at our feet;

With the blessèd Fates to lead us we will laugh and
  sing and play,

And dance the choral dances in our own traditional
  way.

Oh, to us alone is given, when our earthly days are
  done,

To gaze upon the splendour of a never-setting sun;

For we saw the holy Mysteries and heard the god's
  behest,

And were mindful of our duty both to kinsman and
  to guest.

SCENE 2: DIONYSUS *and* XANTHIAS *stand before the
  palace of* PLUTO

[*The* CHORUS *are present, but stand well apart from
the action.*]

DIONYSUS [*approaching the door*]: What sort of a knock should one give, I wonder? [*He raises his hand to knock, but thinks better of it.*] Must conform to local customs, you know.

XANTHIAS: Now come on, don't shilly-shally! Don't forget you're supposed to be Heracles!

DIONYSUS [*knocking timidly*]: Hallo there! Slave!

[*The door is opened by* AEACUS, *the doorkeeper of Hades, a formidable figure.*]

AEACUS: Who's there?

DIONYSUS: Heracles the b-b-bold.

AEACUS: Ah, so it's you, foul, shameless, desperate, good-for-nothing villain that you are. Ought to be ashamed of yourself, you ought! Coming down here, trying to throttle a poor little dog! Poor old Cerberus! I was responsible for that there animal, let me tell you. Well, you're caught now, see? Hah! I'll have you flung over the cliff, down to the black-hearted Stygian rocks, and you'll be chased by the prowling hounds of Hell and the hundred-headed viper will tear your guts out and the Tartessian lamprey shall devour your lungs and the Tithrasian Gorgons can have your

kidneys and – just wait there a moment while I go
and fetch them.

[AEACUS *goes back into the palace.* DIONYSUS
collapses in terror.]

XANTHIAS: Here, what are you doing down there?

DIONYSUS: Dear me, an involuntary libation! Invoke
the god.

XANTHIAS: Stand up, sir, do: somebody might see you.

DIONYSUS: I feel a little faint, Xanthias – I don't feel
very well, really. Here, give me a sponge.

[XANTHIAS *extracts one from the luggage.*]

Press it on my heart, there's a good lad.

XANTHIAS: There you are.

DIONYSUS: No, here. That's it.

XANTHIAS: Heart's slipped a bit, hasn't it, sir?

DIONYSUS: What? Oh, yes, it does that sometimes,
you know. Sudden shock. Gets mixed up with the
lower intestine.

XANTHIAS: Looks like a common case of blue funk
to me.

DIONYSUS: Xanthias, how can you say such a thing?
After I've had the presence of mind to ask you for
a sponge.

XANTHIAS: Very courageous of you, sir.

DIONYSUS: Yes, I think it was, rather. Most people would have been frightened by all those threats and long words. Confess, now, weren't you a weeny bit scared yourself?

XANTHIAS: Didn't turn a hair.

DIONYSUS: Well, if you're feeling so brave and resolute, how about taking my place? Here you are, you take the club and lion-skin. Chance to show your courage. And I'll carry the luggage for you. There!

XANTHIAS: Anything you say, guvnor; you're the boss.

[*They make the exchange.*]

There, how do I look? Reckon the part suits me better than it does you, you old coward!

DIONYSUS: Hm! A very good imitation of a slave dressed up as Heracles. Come on, let me have those bundles.

[*Persephone's* MAID *comes out of the palace.*]

MAID [*to Xanthias*]: Oh, Heracles, dear, how sweet of you to come and see us again! As soon as my mistress heard you were coming she started baking – and there's several cauldrons full of pea soup, and we're roasting a whole ox for you, and

39

she's been making cakes and biscuits – but come along in!

XANTHIAS: Well, thank you very much, but I –

MAID: Nonsense, in you come: the birds are done to a turn, and you should just see the dessert! She's mixed the drinks herself, they're very special. [*She tries to drag him inside.*] Come along, there's a dear.

XANTHIAS: Well, as a matter of fact, I've had breakfast already.

MAID: Don't be ridiculous. I'm not going to let you get away like that. There's such a pretty flute-girl waiting for you inside, and some other girls to dance for you.

XANTHIAS [*rubbing his hands*]: Dancing-girls, eh?

MAID: Hand-plucked, and all in the freshest bloom of middle age. Come in and see for yourself. The cook's just ready with the fish, and the table's laid.

XANTHIAS: Just tell those dancing-girls I'll be with them directly. [*To Dionysus*] Boy, bring the luggage in, will you?

[*The* MAID *goes in.*]

DIONYSUS: Here, wait a minute! Can it be that you are taking my little joke seriously? Just give me back my things and get back to your luggage!

XANTHIAS: *Can it be* that you are thinking of taking back this beautiful lion-skin, after you gave it me and all?

DIONYSUS: I'm not *thinking* of doing so, I *am* doing so. Hand it over, sharp!

XANTHIAS: Well, I'll be –! Ye gods!

DIONYSUS: Gods my foot. Don't you forget that I'm a god and you're not, my boy. You didn't really expect to get away with it as Heracles, did you? Why, you're only a puny mortal!

XANTHIAS: All right, all right, take them. [*Viciously*] If there's ever any other little services I can render . . .

CHORUS:
The moral is plain as plain can be;
As everyone knows who has served at sea,
If you want to be comfy just roll with the ship!
Don't stand like a fool with a stiff upper lip,
But learn from Theramenes, that shrewd politician,
To move with the times and improve your position.

DIONYSUS:

You can hardly expect me to watch my own man
Getting down to the job on a handsome divan
And giving me orders, as likely as not:
'Boy, straighten these covers and bring me the pot!
And take that lascivious grin off your face,
Or I'll teach you a slave should remember his place!'

[*No sooner has* DIONYSUS *resumed the lion-skin than
two* LANDLADIES *enter.*]

FIRST LANDLADY: Come here quick, here's that
scoundrel who came to our inn once and ate up
sixteen loaves.

SECOND LANDLADY: Why, so it is.

XANTHIAS: This isn't going to be nice for somebody.

FIRST LANDLADY: And twenty portions of roast lamb
at half an obol each.

XANTHIAS: Who's going to get it in the neck now?

SECOND LANDLADY: And all those onions.

DIONYSUS: Nonsense, madam, you don't know what
you are talking about.

FIRST LANDLADY: Thought I wouldn't recognize
him, in his lady's boots! – And what about all that
salt fish you had?

SECOND LANDLADY: Yes, and the cheese, fresh that day it was. Wolfed the lot, he did, baskets and all.

FIRST LANDLADY: And when I asked him for the money, oh, you should have seen the look he gave me. Started roaring like a lion.

XANTHIAS: That's him all right. He goes round doing that.

FIRST LANDLADY: Then he comes at me with his sword – I thought he'd gone off his head.

SECOND LANDLADY: Don't blame you, dearie.

FIRST LANDLADY: Oh, he did give us a turn, didn't he, ducks? Had to run upstairs and lock ourselves in. Then, of course, off he went like a streak of lightning. *And* took the best doormat with him.

XANTHIAS: That's right. He never can resist a doormat.

FIRST LANDLADY: Well, we must do something. I know: what about Cleon, he's down here now, isn't he? He'll help us. Run and see if you can find him, will you, dear?

SECOND LANDLADY: Yes, or Hyperbolus – he's passed over too.

FIRST LANDLADY: We'll fix him – look at that great greedy mouth of his – I'd like to knock his teeth down his throat for him, eating us out of house and home!

SECOND LANDLADY: Over the cliff with him!

FIRST LANDLADY: Slit his throat with a billhook!

SECOND LANDLADY: I'll go and find Cleon: he'll have him up in court this very day as ever is.

[*The* LANDLADIES *shake their fists at Dionysus and go out.*]

DIONYSUS: You know, Xanthias, I've grown very fond of you.

XANTHIAS: Ah, no, you don't! I know what you're getting at. I am *not* going to be Heracles again.

DIONYSUS: Dear Xanthias! *Nice* Xanthias!

XANTHIAS: How could I possibly get away with it as Heracles? I'm only a puny mortal.

DIONYSUS: Yes, yes, I know I've offended you, and you've every right to be cross. Look, you take this lovely lion-skin, it suits you beautifully. And if ever I ask for it back, may I rot in Hell, and my wife and children too – and bleary old Archedemus as well, while we're about it.

XANTHIAS: Right! On those terms, I'll do it.
  [*He takes the lion-skin and club, and loads* DIONYSUS
  once again with the baggage.]

CHORUS:
Well, now you're dressed up just the same as before,
  And a sight to make everyone tremble,
You must roll your eyes and swagger and roar
  Like the god you're supposed to resemble.

If you flinch or boggle or muff your part
  And don't talk as brave as you oughter,
You'll be back with the baggage and breaking your
      heart
  'Cos you're only a perishing porter.

XANTHIAS:
  I'm sure you are right: I've been thinking a lot –
    I know my own master, and if he
  Considers there's anything good to be got,
    He'll have all these things back in a jiffy.

  Meanwhile I must practise my vinegar face,
    And throw out my chest and stand steady.
  How's this for a truly horrific grimace?
    (Just in time – someone's coming already!)

[AEACUS *returns, with numerous* SLAVES *carrying whips, ropes, fetters, and instruments of torture.*]

AEACUS: Quick, tie up this dog-stealing bastard and let me give him what he deserves. Get cracking!

[*Two stalwart* SLAVES *bear down on* XANTHIAS.]

DIONYSUS: This isn't going to be nice for somebody!

XANTHIAS [*as* HERACLES]: Hands off, ye dastardly varlets!

AEACUS: Tough, eh? Ditylas! Skobylas! Pardokas! Come here! The gentleman wants a fight.

[*Three more* SLAVES *come forward.*]

DIONYSUS: Ought to be ashamed of himself. Taking other people's things, and then resisting arrest!

AEACUS: Unheard-of effrontery.

DIONYSUS: A hardened criminal.

XANTHIAS: Listen, I've never been here before and I've not stolen so much as a bean belonging to you, strike me dead if I have. I'll tell you what I'll do: I'll let you torture this slave of mine. And if I'm proved guilty, take me off and kill me.

AEACUS [*with relish, and a sharp change of attitude*]: What kind of torture do you suggest, sir?

XANTHIAS: Oh, give him the whole works. Rack,
thumbscrew, gallows, cat-o'-nine-tails: pour vinegar
up his nostrils, pile bricks on his chest – anything
you like. Only don't hit him with a leek or a fresh
spring onion. I won't stand for that – brings tears
to my eyes.

AEACUS: Fair enough. But if he gets damaged
in the process, I suppose you'll be wanting
compensation.

XANTHIAS: No, no, don't worry about that. Just take
him away and do your stuff.

AEACUS: We might as well do it here, under his master's eye. [*To Dionysus*] Come on, put down those
traps, and mind you tell the truth.

DIONYSUS: No, no, look here, you can't – I mean to
say – you can't torture *me*! I'm an immortal. I – I – I
forbid it! If you do, I shall hold you responsible.

AEACUS: I beg your pardon?

DIONYSUS: I'm immortal, I say. I'm a god. Dionysus,
Son of Zeus. And this fellow's a slave.

AEACUS: You hear that?

XANTHIAS: I'll say I do. All the more reason to flog
him: if he's a god he won't feel anything.

47

DIONYSUS: Well, you're a god too, aren't you, Heracles, old man? Why not let them flog you too?

XANTHIAS: Fair enough. Whichever of us squeals first or even bats an eyelid isn't a god at all.

AEACUS: You're a good sport, sir, I can see that. I call that very fair and proper. [*He takes a rope's end from one of the slaves.*] Right! Bend over, both of you.

XANTHIAS: Wait a minute. How are you going to make sure it's a fair test?

AEACUS: Simple. You each get one stroke at a time, in turn.

XANTHIAS: Good idea.

[XANTHIAS *bends over, and* DIONYSUS *reluctantly follows his example.*]

AEACUS [*giving Xanthias a good whack*]: There!

XANTHIAS: I bet you I won't even notice it.

AEACUS: I've hit you already.

XANTHIAS [*incredulously*]: No!

AEACUS: Now for the other one. [*He strikes Dionysus.*]

DIONYSUS: Well, get on with it.

AEACUS: I have.

DIONYSUS: Have you, by Jove? Well, you see? I didn't even sneeze.

AEACUS: Well, I don't know, I'm sure. Let's try the other one again.

XANTHIAS: Come on then!

[AEACUS *whacks him hard.*]

Holy smoke!

AEACUS: What's the matter? Something hurting you?

XANTHIAS: Most provoking! I'd forgotten all about the Festival of Heracles, up at the Diomeia.

AEACUS: Ah! A pious thought. [*To Dionysus*] Your turn.

[*He gives Dionysus another good whack.*]

DIONYSUS: Ow! [*He leaps in the air, with his hands clutched to his bottom.*]

AEACUS: What's the matter?

DIONYSUS: Men on horseback, look! [*He continues to prance about, imitating a man on horseback.*]

AEACUS: Funny they should make you cry.

DIONYSUS: There's a smell of onions.

AEACUS: Sure you didn't feel anything?

DIONYSUS: *Feel* anything? No, not a thing.

AEACUS: Ah, well, we'll have to try the other fellow.

[*He whacks Xanthias.*]

XANTHIAS: Owch!

AEACUS: Aha!

XANTHIAS [*calmly*]: Would you mind pulling out this thorn for me?

AEACUS: What *is* this all about? Well, here we go again. [*He whacks Dionysus as hard as he can.*]

DIONYSUS: Apollo! – h'm, Lord of Delos' holy isle, and something something in the tumty tum –

AEACUS: That hurt him, did you hear?

DIONYSUS: How does it go, now? And something something in the . . . Wonderful poet, Hipponax.

XANTHIAS: You're wasting your time, there's too much padding down there. Try this place here, just under the ribs.

AEACUS: No, I've got a better idea. [*To Dionysus*] Turn round this way. [*He pokes him in the paunch.*]

DIONYSUS [*screaming*]: Poseidon!

XANTHIAS: Somebody get hurt?

DIONYSUS [*singing at the top of his voice*]: . . . king of the mighty deep, Poseidon, lord of the crags and cliffs . . .

AEACUS: I'm blest if I can tell which of you is the god. You'll have to come inside. The master and Persephone'll be able to tell all right: they're gods themselves.

DIONYSUS: I must say I wish you'd thought of that a
bit sooner.

[DIONYSUS *and* XANTHIAS *go in, followed by*
AEACUS *and the* SLAVES.]

CHORUS:

> Come, Muse of the holy dancing choir,
> With wit and charm our songs inspire!
> Here sit ten thousand men of sense,
> A very enlightened audience,
> Who expect a lot of a dancing choir
> And set their hopes of honour higher
> Than CLEOPHON – for he has heard
> The warning of a fateful bird,
> A rather enigmatic swallow
> Whose words, though difficult to follow,
> Should not defy interpretation
> When once translated from the Thracian.
> And this is what the mystic fowl
> Like plaintive nightingale doth howl:
> 'You always vote "agin", but wait!
> Next time – or next – you're *for it*, mate!'

[*The* LEADER *comes forward and addresses the
audience.*]

LEADER:

We chorus folk two privileges prize:
To amuse you, citizens, and to advise.
So, mid the fun that marks this sacred day,
We'll put on serious looks, and say our say.
And first for those misguided souls I plead
  Who in the past to PHRYNICHUS paid heed.
'Tis history now – their folly they regret;
The time has come to pardon and forget.
Oh, yes, they erred, but does it seem quite right,
When slaves who helped us in a single fight
Now vote beside our allies from Plataea
And put on masters' clothes, like Xanthias here –
Not that I disagree with that decision;
No, no, it showed intelligence and vision;
But if we're going to treat these men as brothers,
Let's be consistent and forgive the others.
When we have been so wise, it seems a pity
That men of our own kin, who've served the City
In many naval battles, not just one,
Should still be paying for this thing they've done.
Come, wise Athenians, swallow down your pride!
We need these loyal kinsmen on our side –
As they will be, if every man who fights

Is a full citizen with all his rights.
But if we choose to strut and put on airs
While Athens founders in a sea of cares,
In days to come, when history is penned,
They'll say we must have gone clean round the bend.
CHORUS:
If I've any knowledge of people at all,
I can tell you with confidence what will befall
A rascal with whom we have long been encumbered,
But whose days on this earth, I assure you, are
    numbered.
Though in size he is small, as a bore he's colossal;
Of peace and goodwill he is not an apostle.
He's as fly as a monkey, his voice might be quieter,
And he does very well as a wash-house proprietor.
He is Lord of the Earth, for he sells it in pots
For cleaning the woollies and getting out spots;
He makes up detergents that won't even lather,
For he mixes in ashes to make them go farther.
Yes, CLEIGENES knows that his joys will soon
    cease,
Yet he can't be persuaded to vote for a peace:
He prefers 'the big stick' – for he needs one each
    night

To protect him from thieves when he's rolling home
    tight.

LEADER:

I'll tell you what I think about the way
This city treats her soundest men today:
By a coincidence more sad than funny,
It's very like the way we treat our money.
The noble silver drachma, that of old
We were so proud of, and the recent gold,
Coins that rang true, clean-stamped and worth their
    weight
Throughout the world, have ceased to circulate.
Instead, the purses of Athenian shoppers
Are full of shoddy silver-plated coppers.
Just so, when men are needed by the nation,
The best have been withdrawn from circulation.
Men of good birth and breeding, men of parts,
Well schooled in wrestling and in gentler arts,
These we abuse, and trust instead to knaves,
Newcomers, aliens, copper-pated slaves,
All rascals – honestly, what men to choose!
There was a time when you'd have scorned to use
Men so debased, so far beyond the pale,
Even as scapegoats to be dragged from jail

And flogged to death outside the city gate.
My foolish friends, change now, it's not too late!
Try the good ones again: if they succeed,
You will have proved that you have sense indeed;
And if things don't go well, if these good men
All fail, and Athens comes to grief, why then
Discerning folk will murmur (let us hope):
'She's hanged herself – but what a splendid rope!'

Act Two

SCENE: *Before* PLUTO'S *palace.* XANTHIAS *and an elderly* SLAVE *of Pluto's are engaged on light menial tasks*

SLAVE: Oh, he's a real gentleman, your master is, I can tell that.

XANTHIAS: Yes, you can always tell. There are only two things a real gentleman understands: soaking and poking.

SLAVE: No, but I mean, fancy him not beating you for making out that you was the master and him the slave!

XANTHIAS: He'd have been sorry if he'd tried.

SLAVE: Ah, that's the way I like to hear a slave talking. He, he, he! I love that.

XANTHIAS: Love it, eh?

SLAVE: Why, there's nothing I like better than cursing the master behind his back.

XANTHIAS: Ah, you sly old beggar! I bet you mutter a few things under your breath when he's had a bash at you, eh?

SLAVE: Muttering? He, he, he! Yes, I like a bit of muttering.

XANTHIAS [*encouraging the chuckles*]: And what about prying into his private affairs?

SLAVE: Prying? He, he, he! Yes, I like a bit of prying.

XANTHIAS: Ah, we're going to get along fine, you and me. Have you ever tried eavesdropping when he's got company?

SLAVE: Eavesdropping? Ah, that's real sport, that is.

XANTHIAS: And then you pass it all on to the neighbours, eh?

SLAVE: Well, that's where the fun comes in, ain't it? No end of a kick, that gives me.

XANTHIAS: Put it there, grandpa: give us a hug, that's right. – Listen, my dear old soulmate, my partner in crime, what's all that yelling and shouting and quarrelling going on in there?

SLAVE: That'll be Aeschylus and Euripides.

XANTHIAS: What on earth are they up to?

SLAVE: Oh, there's great goings on among the dead these days, great goings on. Civil war, you might almost call it.

XANTHIAS: What's it all about?

SLAVE: Well, you see, all the fine arts and that, the skilled professions like, there's a sort of custom down here, whoever's the best in each profession, see, he has the right to have his dinner in the Great Hall, with his own chair of honour, up near Pluto, you follow me?

XANTHIAS: I see.

SLAVE: But if somebody else comes along that's better in his profession than what he is, then he has to stand down and let the other feller have the chair.

XANTHIAS: Oh. Well, what is it that's upset Aeschylus so much?

SLAVE: Well, he had the chair for Tragedy, see, because he was the best, like.

XANTHIAS: Who's got it now?

SLAVE: Well, then along comes Euripides, and starts showing off to all the fellers we've got down here – cut-throats, highwaymen, murderers, burglars, regular rough lot they are – and of course he soon has them all twisted round his little finger, with all

his arguments and clever talk and that. And they
all start saying to themselves, 'He's got something,
this bloke,' and getting all worked up, see? So then
Euripides, *he* thinks *he* ought to have the chair
instead of Aeschylus; so he goes and sits in it, and
pushes Aeschylus out.

XANTHIAS: Well, didn't he get flung out on his ear?

SLAVE: Not a bit of it: the people all said *they* had the
right to judge which was the cleverest.

XANTHIAS: What people? All those cut-throats and
pickpockets you were talking about?

SLAVE: Yes, and a devil of a row they kicked up too.

XANTHIAS: Didn't anyone side with Aeschylus?

SLAVE: Well, you see, there ain't many decent folk
down here: just take a look for yourself. [*He indicates the audience.*]

XANTHIAS: What's Pluto going to do about it?

SLAVE: Oh, he's going to have it all done proper, like
a contest, see, and both of them showing their skill,
and proper judging, all legal, like.

XANTHIAS: Just the two of them? Hasn't Sophocles
put in a claim?

SLAVE: Oh, no, when *he* came down here he went
straight up to Aeschylus and took his hand and

59

kissed him like a brother. And Aeschylus says, 'Come on,' he says, 'you must have the chair now,' he says. But Sophocles, he won't hear of it. But now he's sent a message: with this contest coming on, he says, he'll stand by for third man – if Aeschylus wins he'll just go on as before, but if Euripides wins he'll take him on himself.

XANTHIAS: It's really coming off, then?

SLAVE: Any minute now, here where we're standing. [*Confidentially*] They'll want the scales out here, see, for weighing the poetry.

XANTHIAS: Weighing the poetry? I've never heard of a *poet* trying to give short weight.

[SLAVES *emerge from the palace, carrying fantastic pieces of weighing and measuring equipment, and arranging the seating for the contest. Simultaneously, the* CHORUS *makes an unobtrusive entrance.*]

SLAVE: Oh, yes, it's all got to be weighed and measured up proper, with rulers and yardsticks for the words, and compasses and wedges and I don't know what.

XANTHIAS: Regular torture chamber.

SLAVE: Yes, Euripides says he's going to put every line to the test.

XANTHIAS: I reckon Aeschylus must be boiling with rage by this time.

SLAVE: He's been going round all day with his head down, glaring like a bull.

XANTHIAS: Who's the judge going to be?

SLAVE: Ah, that was a ticklish problem: hard to find anyone clever enough. And then Aeschylus said he couldn't see eye to eye with the Athenians anyway –

XANTHIAS: All those burglars and what not. Quite. I see his point.

SLAVE: – and as for the others, he says, none of them could tell a poet from the hind leg of a donkey. So in the end they settled on your master, who's supposed to be a bit of an expert, after all. But we'd better go in: you never want to get in their way when they're busy, it just doesn't pay.

[XANTHIAS *and the* SLAVE *withdraw, as* DIONYSUS *emerges from the palace, looking well feasted and surrounded by* DANCING-GIRLS, ATTENDANTS, *and a company of the* DISTINGUISHED DEAD, *who now take their seats in order to watch the contest. A special throne has been provided for* DIONYSUS, *who is hardly seated before the sounds of angry altercation are heard from the doorway, and* EURIPIDES *and*

AESCHYLUS *appear, arguing heatedly. They are eventually hushed by the assembled company, become conscious of their surroundings, and pay their respects to* DIONYSUS. *The latter motions them genially to take their seats on either side of him. Both are boiling inwardly, however, and during the singing of the ode which follows they continue their quarrel in pantomime. As soon as the ode is finished,* EURIPIDES *bursts into his first intelligible speech.*]

CHORUS:

Ah, how impressive the rage that burns in the heart of the Thunderer!

Vainly the fangs of his rival are bared in a gesture of hate!

Note how superbly he raves, with what fine independence his eyeballs

    In divers directions gyrate!

Words are their weapons: watch out, as the armour-clad syllables hurtle,

Helmeted, crested, and plumed, from the lips of the Poet Most High!

Wait for the clash and the din as the metaphors mingle and jumble,

The sparks as the particles fly!

See the great spread of his mane, as it bristles in
   leonine fury:
No one can doubt any more that those whiskers are
   truly his own!
Huge are the words that he hurls, great compounds
   with rivets and bolts in,
      And epithets hewn out of stone.

Now 'tis the challenger's turn to reply to this verbal
   bombardment:
Neatly each phrase he dissects, with intelligence
   crafty and keen;
Harmless around him the adjectives fall, as he ducks
   into cover
      And squeaks, 'It depends what you mean!'

EURIPIDES [*leaping to his feet*]: I see no reason at all why
   I should withdraw. I happen to be the better poet.
DIONYSUS: What do you say to that, Aeschylus? No
   comment? [AESCHYLUS *remains speechless with rage.*]
EURIPIDES: Isn't that rather typical of the whole
   Aeschylean approach? The majestic silence, the
   pregnant pause?

DIONYSUS: I do feel, Euripides, that you've made rather a sweeping claim, you know.

EURIPIDES: I saw through him years ago. All that rugged grandeur – it's all so *uncultivated*. No restraint. No subtlety at all. Just a torrent of verbiage, stiff with superlatives, and padded out with pretentious polysyllables.

AESCHYLUS [*on the verge of apoplexy*]: Ohh! Well, I suppose that is about the level of criticism to expect from a person of your rustic ancestry. And what are *your* tragedies but a concatenation of commonplaces, as threadbare as the tattered characters who utter them?

DIONYSUS: Now, Aeschylus, aren't we getting a little heated? Calm down!

AESCHYLUS: Not till I've told this – this cripplemerchant where he gets off.

DIONYSUS: Fetch me a black lamb quickly! Stormy weather blowing up.

AESCHYLUS: Not only do you clutter your stage with cripples and beggars, but you allow your heroes to sing and dance like Cretans. You build your plots round unsavoury topics like incest and –

DIONYSUS: Whoa there, stand back! [*He thrusts* AESCHYLUS *firmly back into his seat.*] With all due respect, Aeschylus! Euripides, you poor fellow, wouldn't it be wiser if you moved back out of range a little? I should hate you to get hit on the head by a principal clause and give birth to a premature tragedy. Aeschylus, you must try not to lose your temper. Surely two literary men can criticize each other's work without screaming at each other like fishwives, or flaring up like a forest fire.

EURIPIDES: I'm ready for him! Let Aeschylus have the first word if he likes: I can take it! Criticize what you like – diction, lyrics, plot. I don't care which play you take: *Peleus, Aeolus, Meleager, Telephus* – yes, even *Telephus*.

DIONYSUS: Aeschylus?

AESCHYLUS: I had hoped to avoid having a contest here: it puts me at a considerable disadvantage.

DIONYSUS: How so?

AESCHYLUS: Well, you see, *my* works happen to have outlived me, so I don't have them down here with me. His died with him. But never mind: let's have a match by all means, if you think that's a good idea.

DIONYSUS: Then we must do the thing properly. Bring the brazier and the incense! As the judge of this most, ah, interesting cultural event I must offer up a prayer, before the shafts of wit begin to fly.

[DIONYSUS *rises, takes incense and a libation cup from an attendant and goes to the altar. All present put wreaths on their heads.* DIONYSUS *burns incense and pours a libation.*]

DIONYSUS [*to the Chorus*]: A hymn to the Muses!

CHORUS:

> When men of sage and subtle mind
>> In fierce debate their views do vent,
> And strive some deathless phrase to find
>> To mask each specious argument –
> Then Zeus' virgin daughters nine
> Stand by to watch the sport divine.
>
> Come then today, ye Muses bright!
>> Two grimmer foes ne'er took the field:
> For one is armed with words of might,
>> And one the sword of wit doth wield.
> O heavenly maids, your presence lend!
> The fight is on! Descend! Descend!

DIONYSUS: Now you two must each offer a prayer,
    before we begin.

AESCHYLUS: O Demeter, that didst nourish my brain,
    may I prove worthy of thy Mysteries!

DIONYSUS: And now Euripides: take the censer, it's
    your turn.

EURIPIDES: No, no thank you, I pray to other
    gods.

DIONYSUS: What, special ones of your own? A private
    Pantheon?

EURIPIDES: Precisely.

DIONYSUS: Carry on, then; pray to your lay gods.

EURIPIDES: Hail, Ether, my grazing ground! Hail,
    Pivot of my Tongue! Hail, Mind! Hail, sentient
    Nostrils! Inspire me with all the right answers,
    amen!

CHORUS:

  We're expecting, of course, to pick up a few tips
      From these poets so clever and wise,
  As the elegant vocables fall from their lips
      And their tempers progressively rise.

  Since neither is lacking in brains or in grit
      It should be a most thrilling debate;

67

But while one pins his hopes on his neatly turned
    wit,
  The other relies upon weight.

For shrewd dialectic he cares not a jot;
  And though traps be contrived for his fall
He'll swoop down like a storm and demolish the
    lot –
  Quips, quibbles, opponent, and all.

> [DIONYSUS *and the* TWO POETS *have resumed their
> seats, and the contest begins.*]

DIONYSUS: Right. Off we go. Real, clever, original
stuff, mind – no far-fetched comparisons, no
clichés!

> [*He invites Euripides to begin.*]

EURIPIDES: Before I deal with my own work as a
creative writer, I should like to say a few words
about my opponent. To put it briefly, he is a moun-
tebank and an impostor. Look at the way he cheated
his audience: brought up on Phrynichus, they were
pretty stupid anyway. The play would begin with
a seated figure, all muffled up – Niobe, for example,
or Achilles: face veiled, very dramatic, not a word
uttered.

DIONYSUS: Yes, I remember.

EURIPIDES: Then the Chorus would rattle off a string of odes – four of them, one after the other: still not a syllable from the muffled figure.

DIONYSUS: I must say I rather enjoyed the old silent days. Better than all this talk we get nowadays.

EURIPIDES: That is merely a confession of stupidity.

DIONYSUS: You may be right. But go on. Why did he do that?

EURIPIDES: Well, the whole thing was a swindle, of course. The audience sat there all tensed up, waiting for Niobe to say something. And she just didn't. The play went on, and Niobe sat and sat.

DIONYSUS: Oh, the wretch! D'you know, I never tumbled to that! Now keep still, Aeschylus, what are you fidgeting for?

EURIPIDES: He knows he's beaten. Well, eventually, after a lot more of this nonsense, about half-way through the play we get a speech. And what a speech! A dozen great galumphing phrases, fearsome things with crests and shaggy eyebrows. Magnificent! Nobody knew what they meant, of course.

[AESCHYLUS *utters a moan of rage.*]

DIONYSUS: What *is* that peculiar noise?

EURIPIDES: One just couldn't make sense of anything, it was all –

DIONYSUS [*to Aeschylus*]: Oh, it's you, gnashing your
teeth! Well, don't do it. I don't like it.

EURIPIDES: Scamanders, fosses, shields with brazen
eagle-dragons on them: words that made you dizzy
to hear them.

DIONYSUS: Yes, I once lay awake half the night trying
to figure out what kind of a bird a tawny hippocock
might be.

AESCHYLUS: It was the device painted on the ships,
of course. What ignorance!

DIONYSUS: Oh, I thought it must be another name
for our friend Eryxis.

EURIPIDES: Is a cock of any kind a suitable theme
for tragedy?

AESCHYLUS: And you, you enemy of the gods, what
did you put into *your* plays, may I ask?

EURIPIDES: No hippococks or goatstags, for a start –
or any other mythical monsters from Persian
tapestries. When I took over Tragedy from you,
the poor creature was in a dreadful state. Fatty

degeneration of the Art. All swollen up with high-falutin' diction. I soon got her weight down, though: put her on a diet of particles, with a little finely chopped logic (taken peripatetically), and a special decoction of dialectic, cooked up from books and strained to facilitate digestion. Then I put her on to monodies –

DIONYSUS: With a pinch of Cephisophon.

EURIPIDES: Well, at least I didn't keep rambling on about the first thing that came into my head; or plunge right into the middle of the story and leave everybody guessing. The first character to come on explained the background and origin of the play, straight away.

AESCHYLUS: Lucky he didn't have to explain yours.

EURIPIDES: Then again, as soon as the play began I had everyone hard at work: no one standing idle. Women and slaves, master, young maiden, aged crone – they all talked.

AESCHYLUS: And didn't you deserve to die for your audacity?

EURIPIDES: Not a bit of it. It was Democracy in action.

DIONYSUS: I should keep off that subject, old man, if I were you.

EURIPIDES [*indicating the audience*]: And then, you see, I taught *these* people to talk –

AESCHYLUS: You certainly did, by heaven. If only you had been hacked in small pieces first!

EURIPIDES: I taught them subtle rules they could apply; how to turn a phrase neatly. I taught them to see, to observe, to interpret; to twist, to contrive; to suspect the worst, take nothing at its face value –

AESCHYLUS: You did indeed.

EURIPIDES: I wrote about familiar things, things the audience knew about, and could take me up on if necessary. I didn't try to bludgeon them into unconsciousness with long words, or startle them with characters like Cycnus or Memnon, dashing about with bells on their chariots and rings on their toes. You've only got to look at his disciples, and compare them with mine. He's got Phormisius and Megaenetus, the beard-lance-and-trumpet, tear-'em-limb-from-limb brigade: whereas I have Cleitophon and that smart fellow Theramenes.

DIONYSUS: Theramenes? He's clever all right. Up to anything. Runs into trouble – damn near thing – and what happens? A lucky throw, and up pops Theramenes, well outside the danger zone as usual.

EURIPIDES: What I did was to teach the audience to use its brains, introduce a bit of logic into the drama. The public have learnt from me how to think, how to run their own households, to ask, 'Why is this so! What do we mean by that?'

DIONYSUS: That's right: whenever an Athenian comes home nowadays he shouts at the servants and starts asking, 'Why is the flour jar not in its proper place? What do you mean by biting the head off this sprat? What's happened to that cup I had last year? Where is yesterday's garlic, who's been nibbling at this olive?' Whereas before Euripides came along they just sat and stared idiotically.

CHORUS:

> You hear him, famed Achilles:
> > Be careful what you say!
> Beware lest fury seize you
> > And carry you away.
>
> What though he dares denounce you
> > With taunts and foul abuse?

> To fly into a passion
>   Will not be any use.
>
> So leave your angry fuming
>   And shorten sail instead;
> Wait till the wind blows steady
>   And then go straight ahead.

Come, master of the towering phrase, great poet of
  the age,
Lord of the bosh and balderdash that's talked upon
  the stage,
The time has come for action, flinch or falter you
  must not,
So open up the floodgates, and give him all you've got.

AESCHYLUS: It distresses and pains me to have been
  drawn into an altercation with this fellow. I find
  the whole situation extremely distasteful. But I
  suppose I shall have to reply, or he'll say I'm
  stumped for an answer. Well, I'm going to ask him
  a question. [*To Euripides*] What are the qualities
  that you look for in a good poet?
EURIPIDES: Technical skill – and he should teach a
  lesson, make people into better citizens.

AESCHYLUS: And if you have failed to do this? If you have presented good men, noble men, as despicable wretches, what punishment do you think you deserve?

DIONYSUS: Death. No good asking him.

AESCHYLUS: Well, now, look at the characters I left him. Fine, stalwart characters, larger than life, men who didn't shirk their responsibilities. My heroes weren't like these market-place loafers, swindlers, and rogues they write about nowadays: they were real heroes, breathing spears and lances, white-plumed helmets, breastplates and greaves; heroes with hearts of good solid ox-leather, seven hides thick.

EURIPIDES: There you are! What did I tell you?

DIONYSUS: I hope he's not going to start hammering helmets here.

EURIPIDES: And how did you show the superiority of these characters of yours?

DIONYSUS: Come on, Aeschylus, there's no need to be pompous and difficult.

AESCHYLUS: By putting them into a martial drama.

EURIPIDES: Such as?

AESCHYLUS: Well, the *Seven Against Thebes*, for example. No one could see that play without wanting to go straight off and slay the foe.

DIONYSUS: Well, that was very naughty of you. You made the Thebans so brave they haven't been the same since.

AESCHYLUS: You Athenians could have trained too, only you couldn't be bothered. – Then I put on *The Persians*: an effective sermon on the will to win. Best thing I ever wrote.

DIONYSUS: I loved that bit where they sang about the days of the great Darius, and the Chorus went like this with their hands and cried 'Wah! Wah!'

AESCHYLUS [*ignoring this*]: That is the kind of thing a poet should go in for. You see, from the very earliest times the really great poet has been the one who had a useful lesson to teach. Orpheus gave us the Mysteries and taught people that it was wrong to kill; Musaeus showed us how to cure diseases and prophesied the future; Hesiod explained about agriculture and the seasons for ploughing and harvest. And why is Homer himself held in such high esteem, if not for the valuable military instruction embodied in his work? Organization, training, equipment, it's all there.

DIONYSUS: He doesn't seem to have taught Pantacles much. [*Laughter from the stage audience.*] Of all the clumsy, cack-handed – Do you know, I saw him holding a parade the other day, and he found he had put on his helmet without the crest. There he was, on parade, trying to fix that pony-tail in without taking his helmet off – you should have seen him! [*He gives an imitation.*]

AESCHYLUS [*severely*]: But a lot of excellent men did learn. Look at Lamachus. [*Applause.*] And you can see the imprint of Homer on my own work clearly enough. I depicted men of valour, lionhearted characters like Patroclus and Teucer, encouraging the audience to identify themselves with these heroes when the call to battle came. *I* didn't clutter *my* stage with harlots like Phaedra or Stheneboea. No one can say I have ever put an erotic female into any play of mine.

EURIPIDES: How could you? You've never even met one.

AESCHYLUS: And thank heaven for that. Whereas you and your household had only too much experience of Aphrodite, if I remember rightly. She was too much for you in the end.

DIONYSUS: He's got you there, Euripides. See what happened in your own home, when you made other men's wives behave like that on the stage.

EURIPIDES [*much put out*]: And what harm did my Stheneboeas do to the community, you irritating man?

AESCHYLUS: Why, every decent woman or decent man's wife was so shocked by plays like your *Bellerophon* that she went straight off and took poison.

EURIPIDES: And did I invent the story of Phaedra?

AESCHYLUS: No, no, such things do happen. But the poet should keep quiet about them, not put them on the stage for everyone to copy. Schoolboys have a master to teach them, grown-ups have the poets. We have a duty to see that what we teach them is right and proper.

EURIPIDES: And you think that the right and proper way to teach them is to write your kind of high-flown Olympian language, instead of talking like a human being?

AESCHYLUS: My poor dear fellow, noble themes and noble sentiments must be couched in suitably dignified language. If your characters are demigods, they should talk like demigods – and, I might add, they should *dress* like demigods. I showed the way in this respect; but you have distorted the whole thing.

EURIPIDES: How?

AESCHYLUS: Well, you dress your kings in rags. You make pitiable creatures of them.

EURIPIDES: But why shouldn't I? What harm does it do?

AESCHYLUS [*still serious*]: Well, nowadays you can't get the wealthier classes to pay their naval-defence contributions. They dress up in rags and tell you how poor they are.

DIONYSUS: With nice fleecy underwear underneath. And the next day you see them buying their dinner at the most expensive fish stall in the market.

AESCHYLUS: And then look how you have encouraged people to babble and prate. The wrestling schools are empty, and where have all the young men gone? Off to these infamous establishments where they practise the art of debating – and that

79

isn't all they practise there either. And now even the sailors argue with their officers – why, in my day the only words they knew were 'slops' and 'yo-heave-ho'!

DIONYSUS: Whereas now they refuse to row, and the ship drifts all over the place.

AESCHYLUS: And think of all the other harm he has done. Hasn't he shown us pimps and profligates, women giving birth in temples and sleeping with their brothers and saying that life is not life? Isn't that why the city is so full of lawyers' clerks and scrounging mountebanks, swindling the community right and left? And not a decent athlete left in the whole city – they're all out of training.

DIONYSUS: How right you are! I nearly died of laughing during the torch race at the Pan-Athenian Games. There was a little, fat, white-skinned fellow plugging along miles behind everyone else, making terribly heavy going of it. And when he got to the Potters' Gate and they all ran out and slapped him, here and here and here, the way they do, you know, with the flat of the hand – well, talk about second wind! He produced enough back-draught to keep his torch alight till the end of the race!

CHORUS:

> Fiercely the fight goes on,
>   Doubtful the ending;
> Well matched these warriors are,
>   Grim their contending.
> When one's in full career,
> The other's quick to veer
> And sneak up in the rear
>   To catch him bending.
>
> Yet though you think your gains
>   Are quite extensive,
> Time spent on digging in
>   May prove expensive.
> Show us what wit can do;
> Vary your tactics too;
> Bring out old tricks and new,
>   Risk an offensive.
>
> As for the audience,
>   You are mistaken
> If you think subtle points
>   Will not be taken.
> Such fears are vain, I vow;
> They've all got textbooks now –

> However high your brow,
>> They won't be shaken.
>
> No talking down to these:
>> That's all outdated!
> For native wit alone
>> They're highly rated;
> But now they've learnt to read
> It's real tough stuff they need;
> They don't want chicken-feed –
>> They're educated!

EURIPIDES: Well now, let's turn to your prologues – first things first, after all – and put your famous skill to the test. I maintain that they fail to give a clear picture of the situation.

AESCHYLUS: Which of them do you propose to criticize?

EURIPIDES: Any number of them. But let's start with the opening lines of *The Libation Bearers*.

DIONYSUS: Silence for Aeschylus.

AESCHYLUS [*reciting*]:

Earth-haunting Hermes, that with tutelar eye
Keep'st watch and ward o'er the paternal realm,
Oh, hear my prayer: save me, and be my friend!

Lo, to this land I come and do return.

Do you find anything to criticize in that?

EURIPIDES: A dozen points at least.

DIONYSUS: But he's only recited four lines.

EURIPIDES: With a score of mistakes in each.

DIONYSUS: You'd better not recite any more, Aeschylus: it seems you're four lines down already.

AESCHYLUS: What, stop for him?

DIONYSUS: I think it would be wise.

EURIPIDES: You see, he starts off right away with a preposterous blunder.

AESCHYLUS: Nonsense!

EURIPIDES [*as if washing his hands of the whole subject*]: Oh, well, if that's how you feel . . . It couldn't matter less to me.

AESCHYLUS [*capitulating*]: What is this mistake I've made?

EURIPIDES: Give me those first two lines again.

AESCHYLUS [*reciting*]:

Earth-haunting Hermes, that with tutelar eye
    Keep'st watch and ward o'er the paternal realm –

EURIPIDES: And Orestes says this over the tomb of his dead father?

AESCHYLUS: That is correct.

EURIPIDES: Ah! So he is saying that when his father was brutally murdered by his own wife as the result of a secret intrigue, this all happened under the approving eyes of Hermes?

AESCHYLUS: Certainly not. He is addressing himself to Hermes the Helper, 'earth-haunting Hermes', not to Hermes as the god of trickery. This is made quite clear by the words that follow: 'o'er the paternal realm'. His underground function is a perquisite derived from Zeus, his father.

EURIPIDES: That makes it even worse than I had thought.

DIONYSUS: Underground perquisites, eh? Sounds like a rake-off on the tomb offerings.

AESCHYLUS: A remark in the worst of taste, Dionysus.

DIONYSUS: Give him a bit more, Aeschylus. And you, Euripides, watch out for the mistakes.

AESCHYLUS [*reciting*]:

Oh, hear my prayer: save me, and be my friend!
Lo, to this land I come and do return.

EURIPIDES: The great Aeschylus tells us the same thing twice.

AESCHYLUS: What do you mean, the same thing twice?

EURIPIDES: Well, listen. I'll repeat the line. 'Lo, to this land *I come*', he says, 'and *do return*.' The 'coming' and the 'returning' are the same thing, surely?

DIONYSUS: So they are: like saying to a neighbour, 'Lend me a looking glass – or a mirror would do.'

AESCHYLUS: The two things are not the same. The trouble with you is, you're obsessed with this verbal juggling of yours. The line is a particularly good one.

EURIPIDES: Please explain.

AESCHYLUS: Anyone can 'come' to his native country, if he belongs there still: nothing need have happened to him at all. But when an exile comes home, he 'returns'.

[*Applause from the audience on the stage.*]

DIONYSUS: Well done! What do you say to that, Euripides?

EURIPIDES: I say that Orestes never did 'return' home in that sense: he had to come secretly, he didn't trust the people in power.

[*Frenzied applause from the stage audience.*]

DIONYSUS [*baffled by the applause*]: Brilliant! Brilliant! Wish I knew what you were talking about!

Aristophanes

EURIPIDES: Come on, let's hear some more.

DIONYSUS: Yes, come along, Aeschylus, get on with it. [*To Euripides*] And you, pounce on the howlers.

AESCHYLUS [*reciting*]:

Here on this mound I call on my dead father
To hear me, and to listen.

EURIPIDES: There he goes again, the same thing twice: 'to hear me and to listen'.

DIONYSUS: He's calling on the dead, don't you understand? Even three times would hardly be enough.

AESCHYLUS: And how did you construct *your* prologues?

EURIPIDES: I'll show you. And if I say the same thing twice, or if you find a single word of irrelevant padding, you can spit on me for a liar.

DIONYSUS: Carry on, then. I shall listen most carefully to your choice of words.

EURIPIDES [*reciting*]:

A happy man was Oedipus at first –

AESCHYLUS: Was he at any time? When even before he was born Apollo had decreed that he should

kill his own father? You call that being a happy
man?

EURIPIDES [*reciting*:]

     – But he became the most unfortunate
     Of mortal men.

AESCHYLUS: He didn't become so, he *was* so all along.
Look at his story. First of all, as a new-born baby,
he is dumped out in the cold, cold snow in an
earthenware utensil, to prevent him from growing
up and murdering his father; then he comes limp-
ing to Corinth with both his feet swollen; then he
marries a woman old enough to be his mother; and
then, as though that wasn't bad enough, he finds
out that she *is* his mother. And finally he blinds
himself.

DIONYSUS: Better to have been an Athenian Com-
mander at Arginusae!

EURIPIDES: I still maintain that my prologues are
good.

AESCHYLUS: Even without splitting hairs over every
word, I assure you I can demolish any prologue of
yours with a little bottle of oil.

EURIPIDES: My prologues, with a bottle of oil?

AESCHYLUS: Just one little everyday bottle of oil. You see, the way your prologues are written, you can fit in anything: bottle of oil, pieces of wool, bag of old rag. Tiddly tum. I'll show you what I mean.

EURIPIDES: All right, show me.

DIONYSUS [*to Euripides*]: You must recite one.

EURIPIDES [*reciting*]:

> Aegyptus, who, the oft-told story runs,
> Once put to sea with fifty daughters fair,
> Touching at Argos –

AESCHYLUS: – lost his bottle of oil.

EURIPIDES: What do you mean, lost his bottle of oil? You'll regret this.

DIONYSUS: Recite another prologue. I believe I see the idea.

EURIPIDES [*reciting*]:

> Lord Dionysus of the fawnskin cloak,
> Who leaps with ivy wand amid the pines
> Of fair Parnassus –

AESCHYLUS: – lost his bottle of oil.

DIONYSUS: Two bottles down.

EURIPIDES: He can't keep it up. I've got one here that is guaranteed bottleproof [*reciting:*]

No one is ever fortunate in all:
One man, high-born, loses his wealth; another,
Of lowly birth, has –

AESCHYLUS: – lost his bottle of oil.

DIONYSUS: Euripides!

EURIPIDES: Yes?

DIONYSUS: Reef your sails a bit: this is going to be a
storm in an oil bottle!

EURIPIDES: Don't you believe it. This one'll knock it
right out of his hand.

DIONYSUS: All right, let's have it: but watch out for
bottles!

EURIPIDES [*reciting*]:
    Leaving his native town of Sidon, Cadmus,
    Son of Agenor –

AESCHYLUS: – lost his bottle of oil.

DIONYSUS: If I were you, I'd make him an offer for
the sole rights in his bottle; otherwise you won't
have any prologues left.

EURIPIDES: *His* bottle! I like that! Anyway, I've got
lots of prologues he *can't* fit it into. [*Reciting:*]
    Pelops the Tantalid, with his horses swift,
    Riding to Pisa –

AESCHYLUS: – lost his bottle of oil.

DIONYSUS: You see, he's done it again. Sell it to him, Aeschylus, for heaven's sake. You can get a beautiful new one for an obol.

EURIPIDES: No, no, I've got a lot more prologues yet. [*Reciting*:]

           'Tis said that Oineus –

AESCHYLUS: – lost his bottle of oil.

EURIPIDES: You might at least let me finish one line.

    'Tis said that Oineus, offering to the gods

    Firstfruits of harvest –

AESCHYLUS: – lost his bottle of oil.

DIONYSUS: What, in the middle of a sacrifice? How very awkward for him. Who took it, I wonder?

EURIPIDES: Don't encourage him. See what he can do with this one:

    Almighty Zeus, so Truth herself relates –

DIONYSUS [*anxious to forestall this blasphemy*]: You're beaten, and you know it. That bottle of oil keeps turning up like a stye on the eye. It's time you turned your attention to his lyrics.

EURIPIDES: Ah, yes, those lyrics! Well, I hope to demonstrate that he is a bad lyric writer. His lyrics are all the same.

CHORUS:

What, Aeschylus not write good lyrics?
You'll have the old boy in hysterics!
  I do not know much
  About dactyls and such
(Though I know a good song when I hear it);
  But I had the idea
  That this gentleman here
Was perfection, or something damn near it.
What, Aeschylus not write good lyrics?
Great heavens, what will he say next?
  It seems a bit hard
  On the Eminent Bard –
No wonder he's looking so vexed.

EURIPIDES: They certainly are amazing lyrics, as you'll soon see. I'm going to sing you the whole lot, all in one.

DIONYSUS: And I'll keep the score with these pebbles.
[*Music: flutes, punctuated by deafening crashes on the cymbals.*]

EURIPIDES [*singing*]:
Fiercely the battle is raging: Achilles, thy comrades await thee!

[*Crash!*] Come quickly and help us,
I fear we can hold out no longer!
We who dwell by the lake are proud of our ancestor
Hermes –
[*Crash!*] Come quickly and help us,
I fear we can hold out no longer!

DIONYSUS: Two nasty crashes for you, Aeschylus!
EURIPIDES [*singing*]:
Hearken great lord of the Greeks, and listen to me,
Agamemnon:
[*Crash!*] Come quickly and help us,
I fear we can hold out no longer!

DIONYSUS: That makes three.
EURIPIDES [*singing*]:
Silence! The temple doors open; the virgin priestesses
are chanting:
[*Crash!*] Come quickly and help us,
I fear we can hold out no longer!
Proudly today we march forth, a great and invincible
army:
[*Crash!*] Come quickly and help us,
I fear we can hold out no longer!

DIONYSUS: Which way is the bathroom? I fear I can hold out no longer. You'll have to excuse me – these crashes are bad for my kidneys.

EURIPIDES: You can't go away till you've heard the next part. It has a wonderful lyre accompaniment.

DIONYSUS: Well, get on with it, and no crashes this time, please.

EURIPIDES [*singing*]:

What though the prophet bird with vengeful spear
    Flat-a-thrat-a-flat-a-thrat
The twin-throned kings in muted mockery send
    Flat-a-thrat-a-flat-a-thrat
A fox to dog the Sphinx, a Sphinx to fox the dog
    Flat-a-thrat-a-flat-a-thrat
That through the skies his milky way doth wend
    Flat-a-thrat-a-flat-a-thrat
And, bearing down on Ajax, foxeth *him* –
    Flat-a-thrat-a-flat-a-thrat.

DIONYSUS: What *is* all this flat-a-thrat? A bit of Persian you picked up at Marathon, Aeschylus? Where do you collect all these rope-makers' shanties?

AESCHYLUS: If I make use of traditional elements in my lyrics, I do at least take them from a respectable source and make them serve an artistic purpose. There is more than one kind of flower in the garden of the Muses – why should I have to pluck the same ones as Phrynichus, or anyone else? But this man flings in bits and pieces from all over the place. He gets his inspiration from the brothel or the drinking-club; his lyrics are full of the rhythms of the dance-floor, the dirge-like wailings of these Carian trumpeters. I'll show you what I mean. Bring me a lyre – no, a lyre's too good for this sort of thing: where's that girl with the castanets?

[*A saucy-looking* DANCING-GIRL *comes forward*.]
Aha! The Muse of Euripides! Come along, my dear, stand over here. Just the right accompaniment for this kind of lyric.

DIONYSUS: *Not* in the Lesbian mode, I take it.

[AESCHYLUS *produces a scroll containing his parody of Euripides, evidently prepared beforehand. As he sings the lyric – mimicking the 'modern' style without quite losing his patriarchal dignity – the* CASTANET GIRL *dances.*]

AESCHYLUS [*singing*]:
    Sea birds
Over the wavetops wheeling, chattering,
    Wee birds!
    Wing tips dip,
    Splashing in the –
    Plashing in the –
See how their feathers glisten in the sea-spray –

    Spiders
Up in the rafters, underneath the ceiling,
    Why does
    Each little foot go
    Twiddling and
    Twiddling and –
Busy little weavers working at the loom!

    Dolphin
Plunging, leaping, everybody knows it's a
    Good luck dolphin
    Very fond of music,
Leaping in the bows of a big blue ship.

    Tendrils
Twining, twining, luscious hang the

Clusters on the –
[*the rhythm and tune become repetitive*]
Vine is a –
Grapes on the –
[*here the rhythm changes entirely*]
And I flung my arms around him, and said –
Did you notice that foot?

DIONYSUS [*erotically, his eyes on the castanet girl*]: Yes!
What impudence!

AESCHYLUS: Yes, I thought you would appreciate
that. [*He is pointing out the place in his scroll, but*
DIONYSUS *is unaware of this.*] That initial anapaest
breaks the rhythm completely.

DIONYSUS [*suddenly realizing*]: Oh, yes! Quite.
Absolutely.

AESCHYLUS: A man who can descend to that sort of
thing in his own verse has no right to criticize mine.
Well, so much for his choral songs. Now I want to
give you some idea of what his lyrical monologues
are like. [*Sings:*]
O shining darkness of the Night
Walking forth from the dim shadows of Hades
What is this dream you have sent me?
It has life and yet it has no life

It is a child of the black night
And its face is terrible.
Wrapped in a black shroud it glares at me
Murder, murder in its eye
And it has remarkably long claws.

Light the lamp O my servants
And in your little buckets
Fetch me the limpid liquid
That flows in the mountain streams.
Heat this water (for that is what it is)
I will wash away this dream
That the gods have sent me.

Hearken, O mighty God of the sea –
No, never mind. Hearken, O members of my
    household,
These are great marvels that you have witnessed!
Glycé has stolen the cock from my henhouse
And done a bunk.
Ah, ye nymphs of the mountains –
Or perhaps *you'd* better do it, Manya dear,
Catch her
And bring her to me.

Aristophanes

Ah me, unhappy wretch that I am,
I was just sitting spinning
(Nimble fingers at work on the flax)
And the wheel whirled round and round
And round.
I was going to go out early
While it was still dark,
And sell my thread in the market,
When ah! he did depart, my cock, my treasure;
His soul took to flight,
Winging, winging, into the empyrean
And I was left bereft
To grieve bereaved,
And from my eyes falling, falling,
Tears, the falling tears
Fell, the tears fell, from my eyes fell
Tears.

O Cretans, children of Ida, mighty archers,
Speed to my aid,
Get your bows and arrows
And come round here at once, please, this is
    urgent,
And throw a cordon round the building.

And thou too, daughter of Dictynna,
Fair Artemis, lover of the chase,
Come with your hounds
And we'll track her down yet
If we have to ransack the whole place.
Come then, Hecaté, daughter of Zeus,
With twin torches flaming,
Light me the way across to Glycé's house:
I want to catch the bitch red-handed.

DIONYSUS: I think we've had enough lyrics now.

AESCHYLUS: I've had enough of them too. And I now
propose that we settle this matter once and for all
by a simple test. Let the scales be brought; then
we shall be able to judge whose poetry is the
weightier, his or mine.

[*An enormous pair of scales is brought out, or let
down from above. Meanwhile* PLUTO *appears at an
upper window.*]

DIONYSUS: Come over here, then, both of you, and
I'll be the grocer, weighing out your verses like
pieces of cheese.

CHORUS:

> How thorough these geniuses are!
> But these are the cleverest by far.
> > Did ever you hear
> > Such a brilliant idea,
> So simple, and yet so bizarre?
>
> I'd not have believed it, I swear,
> If a man that I met in the square
> > Had said that a friend
> > Of a friend of his friend
> Had known of a man who was there!

DIONYSUS: Now, each of you stand by one pan of the scales.

[AESCHYLUS *and* EURIPIDES *take up their positions.*]

AESCHYLUS: Right.

EURIPIDES: Right.

DIONYSUS: Now you must each take hold of your own pan and hold it steady, and each recite one line; and when I call 'Cuckoo!' you'll both let go. Ready?

AESCHYLUS: Ready.

EURIPIDES: Ready.

DIONYSUS: All right, speak your lines into the scale.

EURIPIDES: 'Would that the Argo ne'er with wingèd
sail . . .'

AESCHYLUS: 'Spercheios' watery vale, where cattle
graze . . .'

DIONYSUS: Cuckoo!

AESCHYLUS ⎤
EURIPIDES ⎦ *[letting go]*: Right!

DIONYSUS: Oh, look, this side's going *right* down.

EURIPIDES: Now why should it do that?

DIONYSUS: He put in a river. Like the wool mer-
chants: they wet the wool to make it weigh more.
Whereas you with your 'wingèd sails' . . .

EURIPIDES: Well, let's try again. See what he can do
this time.

DIONYSUS: Right, take hold again.

AESCHYLUS ⎤
EURIPIDES ⎦ : Ready.

DIONYSUS: Fire away, then.

EURIPIDES: 'No temple hath Persuasion, save in
words.'

AESCHYLUS: 'Alone of all the gods, Death takes no
gifts.'

DIONYSUS: Let go. Now, let's see – yes, it's this one again. You see, he put in Death; that's a heavy word if you like.

EURIPIDES: Well, what about Persuasion, doesn't that carry any weight? A beautiful line, too.

DIONYSUS: No, Persuasion won't do: mere empty words without sense. You'll have to think of something really ponderous, to weigh your side down. Something strong and big.

EURIPIDES: What have I got that's strong and big? [*A thought strikes him but he rejects it.*] – Umm, let me think.

DIONYSUS: What about that stirring line 'Achilles threw two singles and a four'? Well, come on now, this is the last round.

EURIPIDES [*triumphantly*]: 'He seized his mighty bludgeon, ribbed with iron.'

AESCHYLUS [*triumphantly*]: 'Chariot on chariot, corpse on corpse was piled.'

DIONYSUS: He's licked you again.

EURIPIDES: I don't see why.

DIONYSUS: All those chariots and corpses – a hundred Egyptians couldn't lift that lot.

AESCHYLUS: As far as I am concerned, this line against line business is too easy by far. Let Euripides get into the pan himself, with his children, and his wife, not forgetting Cephisophon of whom we have heard so much, and the whole of his collected works into the bargain. I undertake to outweigh the whole lot with two lines of mine.

DIONYSUS: You know, I like them both so much, I don't know how to judge between them. I don't want to make an enemy of either. One of them is so *clever*, and the other is so *good*, don't you think?

PLUTO [*sepulchrally*]: In that case you've been rather wasting your time down here, haven't you?

DIONYSUS: Well, supposing I do make a choice?

PLUTO: You can take one of them back with you: whichever you prefer. No point in coming all this way for nothing.

DIONYSUS: Bless you! Well now, listen, you two. I came down here for a poet.

EURIPIDES: What do you want a poet for?

DIONYSUS: To save the City of course. If the City isn't saved, there won't be any more drama festivals, and then where shall I be? Now, whichever of you can think of the best piece of advice to give the

Athenians at this juncture, he's the one I shall take
back with me. Now, here's my first question: what
should be done about Alcibiades? Athens is in a
very tricky situation, you know.

EURIPIDES: What do the Athenians think about it,
themselves?

DIONYSUS: Ah. You may well ask. They love him. But
then again they hate him. And then again, they
want him back. But you tell me what *you* think,
both of you.

EURIPIDES [*after consideration*]:
Quickness and brains are what we seek, I know:
He's quick – to harm, but when we need him, slow;
Brilliant enough to plan his own escape,
But useless when the City's in a scrape.

DIONYSUS: That's neat. I like that. Very good. And
Aeschylus, what's your opinion?

AESCHYLUS:
It is not very wise for city states
To rear a lion's whelp within their gates:
But should they do so, they will find it pays
To learn to tolerate its little ways.

DIONYSUS: Honestly, I can't decide between them,
when one's so clever that you can't tell what he

means, and the other's about as clear as the purest mud. We'll try one more question. I want each of you to tell me how you think the City can be saved.

EURIPIDES [*raising his hand*]: I know, sir, please sir, can I speak now, sir?

DIONYSUS: Well, Euripides?

EURIPIDES [*very rapidly*]:

Believe the unsafe safe, the safe unsure,

Mistrust what now you trust, and fear no more.

DIONYSUS: The unsafe safe – I'm afraid that's little bit beyond me, Euripides. Couldn't you give us something a wee bit clearer, not quite so epi— epig— epepig— something not quite so damn clever?

EURIPIDES: It seems perfectly plain to me. If we are now putting our trust in [*mysteriously*] certain persons, and *not* putting our trust in certain other persons, and the City is *not* being saved, then it seems to me that the only reasonable hope of saving the City lies in reversing the procedure. Elementary, my dear Dionysus.

DIONYSUS: Amazing, my dear Palamedes. Well now, Aeschylus, what's your advice?

AESCHYLUS: Tell me, what kind of people *is* the City using nowadays? Presumably they are honest, capable, patriotic –

[DIONYSUS *begins to laugh, gently and not unkindly, but uncontrollably. Soon everyone on the stage except* AESCHYLUS *is helpless with laughter.*]

DIONYSUS: You *are* out of touch, aren't you! No, those are the people she hates most of all.

AESCHYLUS: You mean she prefers dishonest people?

DIONYSUS: She doesn't prefer them, of course not. But she has no choice.

AESCHYLUS: Well, if the City doesn't know its own mind, I don't see how it *can* be saved.

DIONYSUS: You'll have to think of something, if you want to come back with me.

AESCHYLUS: I'd rather reserve my opinion till I get there.

DIONYSUS: Oh, no, you don't: fair's fair. You must send them your good advice from here.

AESCHYLUS: Well, in my day everyone knew the answer:

Treat enemy soil as yours, your own let go:
Your ships are wealth, all other wealth is woe.

DIONYSUS: That's all right, except that the 'other wealth' all goes to the jurymen these days.

PLUTO: Now please decide.

DIONYSUS: Well, in my heart of hearts I have known all the time. No question about it, the man for me is –

EURIPIDES: Now remember you swore by the gods to take me home! [*Emotionally*] Our old friendship . . . you can't go back on an oath!

DIONYSUS [*quoting that fatal line*]: 'My tongue it was that swore . . . ' Come, Aeschylus.

EURIPIDES: What? – Why, what have you done, you unspeakable monster?

DIONYSUS: What have I done? I have declared Aeschylus the winner, that's all. Any objections?

[*Loud applause, in which* PLUTO *joins.*]

EURIPIDES: Can you dare to look me in the face after playing such a low-down, shameful trick?

DIONYSUS: I appeal to the audience.

EURIPIDES: 'Oh, heart of stone, wouldst leave me here to die?' Well, to go on being dead, anyway.

DIONYSUS [*quoting that other fatal line*]: 'Who knows if death be life and life be death?' – And fork be knife, and knife be fork and spoon.

[EURIDIPES, *struggling wildly, is removed by* ATTENDANTS.]

PLUTO [*in his usual sepulchral voice*]: Dionysus and Aeschylus, kindly step inside my palace –

DIONYSUS [*dismayed*]: Why, what have we –?

PLUTO: – where I propose to offer you the hospitality the occasion seems to demand. One for the road, gentlemen, won't you come in?

DIONYSUS/AESCHYLUS [*together, in the same sepulchral tones*]: That's extremely kind of you, Pluto; I don't mind if I do!

[*They enter the palace, followed by the rest of the assembled company.* SLAVES *clear away the seating, etc. The* CHORUS *remain on stage.*]

CHORUS:

How very uncommon it is to find
A man with a shrewd and intelligent mind,
    A man with a sense of proportion!
If you look at the stuff that is written today
And the stupid things our statesmen say,
You would think that people had lost the knack
Of telling the white from the utterly black –
    They've thrown away all caution!

They sit at the feet of Socrates
Till they can't distinguish the wood from the trees,
   And tragedy goes to POT;
They don't care whether their plays are art
But only whether the words are smart;
They waste our time with quibbles and quarrels,
Destroying our patience as well as our morals,
   And making us all talk ROT.

So altogether we're glad to find
That a man with a shrewd and intelligent mind
   (A man with a sense of proportion)
Is returning to Earth, as this comedy ends,
To the joy of his colleagues, relations, and friends –
Is returning to Earth, in this decadent age,
To save the City and save the stage
   From politics, lies, and distortion.

> [PLUTO *and his* GUESTS *come out of the palace, and
> the* 'DEAD' *who have formed the audience on the stage
> gather round to see them off.*]

PLUTO: Good-bye, then, Aeschylus, off you go with
your sound advice and save the City for us. Educate
the fools – you'll find a good many. And give this
[*he hands him a vicious-looking knife*] to Cleophon

with my compliments, and these [*a pair of nooses*] to the Tax Commissioners, and here's one for Myrmex and another for Nicomachus; and this [*a bowl labelled 'Hemlock'*] is for Archenomus: and tell them all to hurry up and come down here to me. Otherwise I shall brand them and tie them together by the feet along with Adeimantus, and have them packed off underground before they can say knife.

AESCHYLUS: Very well, I will. And will you, please, ask Sophocles to take over my Chair of Honour and look after it while I am away? I declare that the second place is his by right. And on no account must that wicked, lying, foul-mouthed scoundrel ever be allowed to sit on my chair, even inadvertently.

PLUTO [*to the Chorus*]: Guide him, then, with your sacred torches, escort him with his own songs and dances.

[*The* CHORUS *form up as an escort for* AESCHYLUS, *and the procession moves off, singing.*]

CHORUS:

> Spirits of the darkness,
>   Speed him on his way;

Safely may he journey
  To the light of day.

To the City's counsels
  May he wisdom lend;
Then of war and suffering
  There shall be an end.

If those doughty warriors,
  Cleophon and Co.,
Want to keep on fighting,
  They know where to go.

In their distant homeland
  They can do less harm;
Let them wage their warfare
  Back on father's farm.